# *Sex Questions For Couples*

## Ignite Your Desire With Hot Talk

Michael and Barbara Kortekaas

Succulent Enterprises Inc.

# Dedication

This book is dedicated to all couples striving to create a loving, long lasting relationship that is filled with joy and happiness. We hope this book inspires you to creatively enhance your relationship with even more fun and pleasure. Stay frisky and playful as you grow even closer together.

# Play Safe

Always use safer sex practices and common sense when performing or engaging in any sexual activity. Sample activities provided are designed for couples in a monogamous sexual relationship. All the foreplay and sex play ideas are intended to inspire your own sexual creativity so you can enhance your relationship with more pleasure and intimacy. They are only sexy suggestions for you to adapt and perform at your own discretion.

**Special Note**: always clean before inter-mixing anal then vaginal activities to avoid bacterial infections. Also avoid getting anything with sugar in the vagina. This can lead to a nasty yeast infection.

# Fun Sex Questions

Everyone wants an exciting and satisfying sex life. One filled with erotic adventures, stimulating sensations, romantic intimacy and creative foreplay. If you want more excitement in your relationship, you can be sure your partner does too. They may not show it but you know their passion is just waiting for the right spark to ignite the fires of their lust.

When you want to add more sizzle into your sex life, you need to find out what get's you both hot. Do either of you have any secret sexual desires smoldering on the back burner? Are there other erotic ideas that will catch alight and burn bright in your relationship? What will inspire you both to fan the flames of your love so it blazes with intense passion and excitement? Discovering the answers to these questions requires even more steamy questions. But with the right inspiration, you'll be able to start your sexual fires burning in no time.

This book has 469 fun sex questions that will help stoke your desire with creative new ideas for being naughty, frisky and playful. Use them any time to stimulate thought provoking discussions that will arouse both your mind and body together. Tease and tantalize each other with hot talk as you reveal your answers and inflame your craving for each other.

All the sex questions in this book are for fun and for play. Start a sexy conversation about different types of intimate ideas and see where it leads. When you feel more comfortable talking about sex together, you'll feel much more comfortable enjoying sex too.

# Why Sex Questions?

Sex is extremely important in a loving relationship. Physical intimacy helps strengthen your connection and emotional bonds. Although sexual chemistry plays a big part in attracting couples together initially, once you're in a committed relationship you need more. Making love together becomes better as you develop more trust and start enjoying emotional intimacy in combination with your sensual pleasures. Creating a bond deeper than just friendship requires an understanding and awareness of both yourself and your partner. Shared experiences, including foreplay and sex, give you opportunities to learn about each other and pick up nonverbal clues about your partner's personality. But to get at your real desires and needs, you must have meaningful conversations one on one.

Unfortunately, talking about intimate or sensitive subjects like sex can be difficult for many people. Our conversation skills tend to be focused more on socializing with friends or interacting with coworkers. Many people have trouble expressing their true feelings and are shy or nervous about revealing their real sexual needs. It can be hard to ask for what we want sexually especially with someone we care about. Social conditioning may inhibit how we express ourselves but we all have needs that can only be satisfied when shared with our partner. To feel really fulfilled, understood and appreciated by your partner, you need to have intimate and ongoing conversations about a broad range of topics. To become sexually satisfied, you need to talk to each other about your sexual desires whatever they may be.

Many couples may have talked about sex to some degree while dating and assume they know what their partners want. But as you gain more experience in life, love and sex, you also grow your expectations and desires. What may have been novel and thrilling when you were younger may now be considered vanilla or plain. As you become more comfortable with yourself and your partner, you may be willing and eager to explore more sophisticated sexual experiences. But unless you communicate these new desires, your partner may never realize that your love life is becoming routine or boring. And it may be happening for them too. Both of you may be eager to explore new sensual pleasures together while being fearful of discussing any ideas for change. This type of situation is such a shame and it affects so many couples. To ensure your relationship doesn't fall into this trap, you need to get a conversation started. This book is a valuable resource that will help guide you through a series of intimate questions while you build your confidence and trust in each other.

Even if you've been married for many years, these fun questions will help you discover even more about what and how your partner thinks of your love and sex life. They'll help you express your desires and even encourage you to discover more about yourself in the process. Start talking about sex together. You'll both be glad you did.

# Playing With Sex Questions

In this book you'll discover a broad range of fun sex questions to discuss with your partner. Although extremely important, we've tried to keep the serious types of sex questions for a different book. We want these questions to help you focus on the fun side of your relationship. So when you're both in a playful mood, use these intimate questions to explore how you can spice up your love life with more creative sexual pleasure. Once you both feel comfortable talking about sex, any serious questions you have will be much easier to explore together later.

All the questions in this book are intended to inspire your sexual creativity. They'll encourage you both to think about sex more often and in different ways. You'll come up with hot new ideas and recall others that you've tried and now want to try again. When answering each question, be as honest as you can be with both yourself and your partner. Say what first comes to mind without trying to censor yourself. Watch for each other's reaction to each question. Also be as encouraging as you can be when listening to your partner's responses. When you're supportive and appreciative, they'll be much more willing to reveal and explore all their secret sexual desires.

We've included different styles of questions. Some are multipart that include related questions to help expand on the idea. There are some questions with multiple options for completing them. When asking your partner one of these style of questions, you can go through all the options or just pick one of them and leave the other options to be asked later. There are also either/or style questions. When answering these, indicate your choice but also give some explanation as to why you chose it. You'll also find questions phrased for a yes or no type response. Follow these up with a request to explain thoughts or feelings about the answer or give your own feedback to keep the discussion going. Try to elaborate and discuss the details as much as you feel comfortable.

Some questions may shock and surprise you while others will encourage you to examine your beliefs and assumptions about each other. Most questions are intended to be gender neutral so specific references to penis, clitoris, vagina, etc. are left out on purpose. In this way, you can both ask and answer each question from your own perspective.

Although grouped into sections, we've mostly randomized the questions so you can go through them in sequence from 1 to 469 if you desire. It's best to alternate asking and answering the questions. If you're talking on the phone or driving together, the person with the book can both read the question aloud and answer it on their turn if necessary.

Here are a few other ways you can play with these sex questions:

- Ask your partner to pick a number from 1 to 468 (leave the last one for later) and look up the matching question to ask them. Then switch with you selecting a random number. Continue until you come up with a sexy idea you can't wait to try out.

- Randomly pick a page then roll a single die to determine which question on the page to ask. If the die number is greater than the number of questions on the page, you get to make up your own question to ask.

- Roll one or two dice and use the number rolled to determine the first question. Switch and roll the dice again. This time add the roll to the last number to determine the next question. Continue until you get to the final question.

- When playing any game with points, every time you gain points, ask or answer the question corresponding to your current score. Depending on the game, multiply your score by some number to sample the full range of questions. Use the question and answer corresponding to the winning score to come up with a sexual reward.

- When driving together on a long trip, choose the license plate number of a passing car and use the numbers and letters in some way to determine which questions to ask. Alternate until you get to your destination or need to pull over for some fun.

- When it's your turn to answer a question from the book, also come up with your own question for your partner that is related to or follows on from the one you just finished.

Although intended for two lovers to play together, you can add to the erotic fun by playing with other couples too. If it's your turn to ask the question, choose an appropriate person to answer based on the nature of the question. You can even ponder them solo to discover your own feelings and desires.

Note that some questions may seem very similar but the wording is different which affects how you think about it. You're also likely to get wildly different answers and follow up discussions even when you re-ask a question at some other time. The more you play with these sex questions, the more insight you'll gain about both of your attitudes, preferences and desires.

Remember, this book is designed to be used when you and your partner are feeling playful and not when you're looking for relationship therapy. But having amazing sex together is great for any relationship. We hope you have fun with this book and discover lots of ways to enjoy each other.

# Things to Consider

We've included intimate questions from a variety of categories related to your sex life. Here are a few extra things to consider about using sex questions to stimulate your hot talk.

## Fabulous Foreplay

Foreplay is an extremely important part of an intimate sexual relationship. But the type and quantity of foreplay that we desire changes all the time. In some situations very little physical stimulation may be required to become aroused because you've both used "mental foreplay" to get excited leading up to your sexual encounter. At other times, the stress of the day may require a wind down period of relaxing sensual pleasure before making love together. To feel fully satisfied, an orgasm is not always enough. The quality time together enjoying mutually shared pleasures is what makes for an emotionally fulfilling sex life. Emotional intimacy also involves a range of feelings from affectionate caring to intense passion to naughty fun. By asking intimate questions about various types of foreplay pleasures, you can identify your individual preferences and expectations. You'll discover ways that you can make foreplay even more fun for both of you before, during and after sex.

## Mental Foreplay

Your brain is your biggest sex organ. It controls your level or excitement and how you respond to arousing stimulation. It can also distract you with unpleasant thoughts and emotions that can totally ruin a night of great sex. But, if you use the right types of mental foreplay, you can get your brains in on the action. There are many ways to turn each other on without physically touching. Erotic sights, sounds, tastes and smells can all be used in various combinations to get your lover thinking about hot sex with you. You can even send each other erotic text messages throughout the day to get your passion fires burning. The trick is discovering what your partner wants and needs to get turned on.

**Fantastic Fantasies**

Fantasies come in various forms from elaborate mental stories to quick thoughts of a sexual encounter. You can have a sexy day dream or erotic thought at any time of day. Like mental foreplay, imagined fantasies can arouse your desire and lust for each other. They can make sex and masturbation even more exciting and can help intensify your orgasm. The great thing about fantasies is that they can be wildly fanciful or involve impossible scenarios. In your mind, you're free to be as kinky as you want and indulge in any form of deviant activity you desire. Sexual fantasies can be a healthy and important part of your sex life together. However, they can also be extremely sensitive and deeply personal. So rather than asking "Do you have sexual fantasies?", focus on exploring different types of sexy ideas, erotic thoughts and wild possibilities. Creatively using your imagination together to come up with new and playful activities can lead to a more satisfying and fulfilling relationship.

**Positively Pornographic**

For good or bad, porn and other forms of erotica are part of our world. Stories and images of sex serve as both entertainment and education. People are fascinated by sex so it's not likely to go away nor should it. It affects how and what we learn about sex, what we desire, what we believe and how we act. Some aspects of our sexual behaviour and expectations are influenced by our experiences with porn. Couples can benefit from using porn and other erotica in their relationship. It can be a fun way spice up your relationship and discover new ways to play together. Start a conversation with some fun sex questions about porn and discover how you can turn each other on.

## Vivid Colors

"What's your favorite color?" is a basic ice breaker question because color really is important to us. Color makes life interesting. It also affects our emotions in various ways. But of course we don't usually have just one favorite color. It depends on what thing the color applies to. Have some fun with sex questions involving color to add a bit of spice to your private conversations. Discover how to make your intimate times more vivid by adding a splash of sexy color to your love play.

## Dirty Words

When it comes to sex, words can be emotionally loaded. One word could turn you on while another might turn you off totally. Knowing which one to use when talking sexy can be important. Swear words and even derogatory slang can play a role in hot dirty talk but the choice of words can be critical. During the throes of passion, some women may get off being called a slut while others would cringe in disgust. Bitch may resonate with some women while for others it's demeaning. Do you like to get laid, screwed, fucked or made love to? Do you prefer terms like going down, sucked off, eaten out, blow job or more clinical words like cunnilingus and fellatio? Like a mental minefield, it's important to discover what words your lover prefers so you can trigger the intended reaction. We've included some questions to help you discover different words and phrases for sex, body parts, kinky activities, swear words, getting hot and making love. Once you discover which words turn you on, you can explore new ways for using them to get each other even more excited.

# Romantic Revelations

*When you're in a relaxed state before or after making love, softly caress your lover and entice them to reveal their romantic desires. Communicate pleasures that each of you wish to experience. Explore each other's special cravings that would make life that much more enjoyable. Discover each other's fantasies and discuss ways that they can be fulfilled.*

## 1

Everyone has secret sexual desires that they believe are too sensitive, shocking or weird to reveal even to their partner. What can I do to help make you feel more comfortable sharing our secret desires so we can both satisfy them together?

## 2

Some people think sexual fantasies should stay secret while others believe that it can be fun to reveal them and even turn them into reality. How do you feel about exploring and sharing our sexual fantasies?

## 3

What aspect of our lovemaking do you like the best? What is your favorite erotic memory of our time together?

## 4

How important is foreplay to you for great sex? What makes for good foreplay?

## 5

If you were given the chance to "see" all the sexual thoughts, dreams and fantasies of just one person, whose mind would you want to read?

## 6

What is the "strangest" fantasy you enjoy and will admit to, but would never or could not actually do in real life?

## 7

How kinky or sexually adventurous do you feel:

    You are?
    I am?
    We could be?

## 8

How curious about sex were you as a kid? What kinds of things did you do to satisfy your curiosity?

# Fabulous Foreplay

*Use your creativity to engage your lover in a complete sensual experience that exhilarates their entire body and mind. Provide a feast for all five senses. Allow time to savor an entire range of sensory delights. When you make love next, strive to make foreplay absolutely fabulous.*

## 9

How do you think we can make foreplay more fun? How would you most like to spice up our foreplay?

## 10

How do you feel about experimenting with creative new foreplay techniques? What new types of foreplay would you enjoy trying?

## 11

How do you feel about being blindfolded while I surprise you with pleasure? What types of foreplay techniques have you experienced while blindfolded?

## 12

How do you feel about watching porn together as foreplay?

# 13

Suppose we were making a penis mold that takes a while to set. How long do you think "we" could maintain an erection and what types of stimulation do you think would be required to keep it hard?

# 14

Do you prefer to be spontaneous in what we do as foreplay or plan it out? In what ways do you like to mix up your foreplay moves?

# 15

What is your favorite foreplay technique that:

You use to pleasure me?
I use to pleasure you?

# 16

If we were to play out a modern day fantasy or role playing scenario, would you rather be:

Doctor or patient?
Escort or client?
Executive or assistant?
Cop or criminal?
Photographer or model?

# Kiss Connection

*The way a person kisses is a good indicator of how they make love. Improve your kissing style and range of techniques and you will inevitably improve your skill as a sensual lover. Even in established relationships, never take kissing for granted. Learn to kiss well and practice often. Combine different types of kisses in erotic patterns of sensual delight. Connect with your lover through the art of kissing.*

# 17

How important is kissing to you? How can someone learn to be a better kisser?

# 18

In what ways do you feel we can improve the way we kiss each other? How can I improve the way I kiss you?

# 19

Where do you most like to be kissed other than on the lips?

# 20

What color lipstick do you think is most kissable? What color of lipstick do you think is the most erotic for oral sex?

# 21

Would you rather redo or relive the first romantic kiss you ever had? How do you think we can recreate the exciting sexual curiosity of our first make out sessions?

# 22

Have you ever had or given someone:
An electric kiss?
An upside down kiss?
A vampire kiss or hickey?
A snowball kiss?

# 23

How did you first learn to kiss? What else do you feel we could learn about kissing?

# 24

What makes for a great kiss? What styles of kissing do you enjoy most?

# Erogenous Exploration

*With your lips and tongue, explore your lover's entire body.
Resist the urge to concentrate on areas you already know.
Map out new territory. Add some warm and cool breaths to
further stimulate sensitive areas you discover.*

## 25

What do you think are my most sensitive
erogenous zones? Which part of my body
do you most enjoy stimulating?

## 26

During foreplay, which of your erogenous
zones or parts of your body would you like
me to:

Touch and caress more?
Kiss and lick more?
Rub and massage more?
Stay away from?

## 27

With someone of the same sex, how would
you feel about:

French kissing?
Performing a handjob?
Receiving a handjob?
Receiving oral sex?
Performing oral sex?
Having sex together?

# 28

How many different types of nipple stimulation can you think of? What forms of nipple stimulation do you enjoy most?

# 29

What household items can you imagine using to pleasure each other? What would we do with them?

# 30

What is the most imaginative foreplay technique you have ever experienced or heard of?

# 31

How would you most like to tease and tantalize me during our sex play?

# 32

In what ways do you think we can make our sex play more creative and erotically adventurous?

# Luscious Lips

*Wild and hungry or feather soft, use your lips to arouse your lover in ways they least expect or longingly desire. Explore their body for hidden erogenous zones or revel in a sensuous kiss. Keep your lips soft for all occasions.*

## 33

What is your best tip or technique for performing great oral sex on:

A man?
A woman?

## 34

If I was naked and pretended to be a statue standing perfectly still, what would you do with just your tongue to make me move?

## 35

How do you feel about kissing after receiving oral sex?

## 36

What color would you associate with the word:

| | |
|---|---|
| Love? | Sensual? |
| Sexy? | Passion? |
| Luscious? | Delicious? |
| Nasty? | Kinky? |

# 37

How often would you prefer me to perform oral sex for you as:

Foreplay?
Your climax?

# 38

How do you feel about role reversal and gender play? What kinds of scenarios can you imagine us role playing?

# 39

What is one foreplay technique you would like to try that we have not done yet? What is one sexual activity you would like to try that we have never done before?

# 40

If we were both sentenced to house arrest together for 6 months with no other responsibilities, what kinds of things do you think we would order online to make sure our sex play never got boring?

# A Loving Touch

*Use your fingers as delicate instruments of pleasure. Lovingly touch and stroke your lover's entire body. Sensitize their skin as you slowly explore for new erogenous zones. Take your time teasing and tantalizing until their genitals tingle with desire.*

# 41

What forms of affection and non-sexual intimacy do you want more of in our relationship?

# 42

In your opinion, how is having sex different from making love?

# 43

What is your best foreplay tip if you were giving advice to:

A woman?          A man?
A lesbian?          A gay guy?

# 44

Are there any foreplay habits or routines that we have that you feel need a make over?

## 45

What sex toys do you have that you want me to use with you during our sex play?

## 46

Have you ever been involved in a threesome or more-some? If we were going to have another person or couple join us, who would you want to get together with and how would you imagine us doing it?

## 47

If we were to receive a prize for the most amazing sex scene, what would we have been doing together?

## 48

Think of a love story we've both seen together recently that had a happy ending. If you had to "finish" the movie with a sex scene, in what setting would the scene take place and what would the characters be doing?

# Library of Love

*Making love can be an art form when you fine tune your skills. Becoming a master of intimacy requires lots of practice combined with knowledge and a desire to learn. Invest in a private library of love. Learn creative techniques beyond your imagination. Discover ideas for new fantasies. Gain confidence as you discover the joy of learning. Buy a new book of love for your collection today.*

## 49

What types of things do you do to improve your knowledge about sex?

## 50

What is your favorite type of erotic reading material?

## 51

In a fantasy or role playing scenario set in ancient times, would you rather be the:
Priest or worshiper?
Knight or the one rescued?
Barbarian or missionary?
Witch or inquisitor?
Traveler or native?

## 52

If we were to write an erotic story together, what would it be about?

# 53

What forms of sex education did you receive and how are you continuing to learn more?

# 54

If you had started a sexual scrapbook or memory box when you were a teenager, what kinds of things would you have put in it?

# 55

When it comes to playful activities that we can enjoy together:

Where do you get your sex play ideas?
Where is the best place to find creative ideas?
How can we come up with new ideas to try?

# 56

If you could go back in time to take photos or videos of your sexual history, what key events in your love life would you want to record?

# 57

Are there any foreplay skills you feel we need to learn or relearn?

# Control of the Zone

*When you master the erogenous zones of your lover, you will control awesome powers of pleasure. Wielding these powers to stimulate your lover with wonderfully subtle or intense sensations is a joy in itself. Watching them squirm in ecstasy as you control every nuance of their pleasure is extremely arousing. Take time to learn: explore and experiment, tease and test, seduce and study.*

## 58

What are your most ticklish erogenous zones?

## 59

For mysterious reasons you wake up with a mixture of gender traits. Which mixture would you rather have?

A: Feminine features including breasts but with a penis and testicles

B: Masculine features but with a vagina and clitoris

## 60

Suppose you magically switched gender one night but kept all your existing personality traits. If you knew this was permanent, would you want to switch to an opposite sex partner (your previous sex) or "turn" gay?

# 61

What's the strangest thing you've done or thought about to avoid a premature ejaculation?

# 62

Would you ever consider timing ourselves to determine the fastest time to:

Strip and get into position?
Have a quickie?
Get an erection?
Perform oral sex?
Finish a hand job?
Have a G-spot orgasm?
Masturbate to orgasm?
Get into ten sex positions?

# 63

Have you ever gone sex toy shopping with a lover? While there, have you ever:

Squeezed a realistic dildo (texture & shape)?
Fingered a fake pussy to see what it feels like?
Tested a vibrator intensity on your nose?
Imagined fitting in the largest dildo they had?
Considered a sex doll for a pretend threesome?
Bought more than one sex toy at one time?

# Tongue in Cheek

*The perineum and anus contains many nerve endings that are very receptive to stimulation. Using your tongue, you can make your lover squirm in ecstasy. Although a taboo area, let your lover know that your desire to lick and kiss their ass is more than a tongue in cheek expression. A dental dam with a dab of lubricant on both sides will help reduce any inhibitions.*

## 64

How do you feel about anallingus? Have you ever performed or received a rim job?

## 65

Have you ever gagged and puked while performing oral sex?

## 66

What color of condoms have you used before or would like to try? Are there any specific brands or types of condoms that you prefer? Have you ever had sex using a female condom?

## 67

If you had to give names to your favorite sex toys, what would you call each of them? Have you ever given a name to one of your sex toys?

# 68

A radical new law requires all marriages to involve three people instead of two. Which type of arrangement would you prefer and who would you want to join us?

A: Two men and one woman
B: Two women and one man

# 69

For some reason, you have to watch me have sex with someone else but you get to choose the person and the activities we perform together. Who would you select and what would you have us do if it had to involve:

An opposite sex partner?
A same sex partner?
Another heterosexual couple?
A lesbian couple?
A gay couple?

# 70

Have you ever discovered anyone sniffing your panties or underwear?

# 71

What kinds of kinky sex accessories do you own? Have you ever made any?

# Backdoor Intruder

*Anal play is a naughty pleasure both women and men can enjoy regardless of sexual orientation. Use lots of lubrication with your anal toys and be very gentle. All anal toys should have a flared base to ensure they don't get lost.*

## 72

How do you feel about ass play and anal pleasuring? What types of ass play would you enjoy as part of our sexual fun?

## 73

How do you feel about anal stimulation while receiving oral sex?

## 74

What is the kinkiest thing you can imagine us doing together in a fantasy?

## 75

Suppose that every time we finish having anal intercourse together, my/your vagina transforms into a fully working penis. This new penis must then be used for anal intercourse to revert back to normal. How would this affect your desire for anal sex?

# 76

As part of our sex play, how would you creatively use:

   A butt plug or anal dildo?
   A vibrator or dildo?
   A double dildo or strap-on?

# 77

Have you ever:

   Used a special prostate massager?
   Used a glass or steel butt plug?
   Used a vibrating butt plug?
   Had intercourse with a butt plug inserted?
   Gone out with a butt plug inserted?

# 78

What kind of erotic story or fantasy can you think of that involves:

   A magic dildo?
   A twisted sex genie?
   A time machine?
   A kinky witch?
   A sexy "monster"?

# 79

If we role played as space aliens, what non-human color and texture of skin would you find attractive?

# Brush With Bliss

*Get a few soft artist brushes. She lies naked, blindfolded. Pretend the brush is a butterfly. Start on the soles of her feet then each toe, ankle, calf, knee. Flit to her arm pit, face, breasts. Fly to her inner thighs, perineum, vulva. Delicately quick, linger, pause. Random touches tantalize and tingle. Dip a longer brush in aromatic oil. Swirl and spiral around her nipples and clitoris.*

## 80

What creatively sensual activities can you imagine doing to each other with:

An artist brush?      A flower?
A feather?            Silk scarves?

## 81

How did you react the first time you saw:

A flaccid penis grow erect?
A penis ejaculate?
A female ejaculation?
Someone going down on you?
The opposite sex peeing?

## 82

When it comes to naughty playthings, have you ever:

Been caught masturbating with toys?
Caught anyone using your toys?
Discovered toys from friends or relatives?
Been caught using toys that aren't yours?

# 83

What types or styles of erotic art do you enjoy the most?

# 84

Which would you rather have as a lunch time quickie?

A: Oral sex
B: Intercourse

# 85

Have you ever used or would you like to try using a:

Penis extension?     Cock ring?
French tickler?      Penis pump?

# 86

What kinds of things do you think you could find in a hardware or home renovation store that we could use to enhance our sex play? What would you do with them?

# In The Spot Light

*Star in your own erotic video. Write a script together that plays out a favorite fantasy or parody an existing movie. Improv if you want. A strip tease or bathroom scene can be an erotic starting point. Or, just hit record and ravish each other's bodies. Use the night shot mode if desired. Have fun making the movie then enjoy watching it over and over again.*

## 87

If we were to make our own erotic video for just the two of us, what would be the setting, theme or plot of the movie and what kinds of sex play would we film?

## 88

How do you feel about taking digital pictures of each other and using a graphics program to make our own collection of erotic art?

## 89

What kind of money shot do you find is the most erotic? Do you prefer to see the guy pull out to ejaculate or see a "cream pie"?

## 90

Who do you think is the most sexually arousing movie star and in what role?

# 91

How would you feel about filming one of "our" ejaculations so we can watch it in slow motion?

# 92

Have you ever fantasized about being a porn star? What porn star names would you create for each of us?

# 93

Think of the characters and scenarios in your favorite television shows. Which ones would you most like to role play?

# 94

If you were a porn director "interviewing" me for a new movie, what kinds of things would you want demonstrated on the casting couch?

# 95

What kinds of erotic movies would you find interesting to watch together? Are there any that you prefer to watch alone for any reason?

# More Than a Mouthful

*For women who like to have their breasts and nipples caressed, licked and sucked, it's hard to lavish too much attention on them. Use your fingers and mouth to stimulate her entire breast not just the nipple. Remember to switch sides every now and again to keep them both happy and she'll be eager for more. Some women can even have orgasms from breast stimulation alone.*

## 96

Have you ever been able to have an orgasm by stimulation of any erogenous zone other than your genitals? Can you show or tell me how to give you this type of orgasm or would you like to try to find a way to make it happen together?

## 97

Have you ever received or performed cunnilingus and discovered it was that time of the month? Would you still consider enjoying oral-clitoral stimulation at this time?

## 98

Would you use a dildo that could ejaculate warm lube or another tasty substance? What flavor?

# 99

Of the sexual features you've ever seen personally on a woman, how big was the biggest:

Pair of boobs?    Nipple?

Bush?    Clitoris?

# 100

What flavor of jam would make toes more tasty for you?

# 101

Of the sexual features you've ever seen personally on a man, how:

Big were the biggest balls?

Long was the longest penis?

Wide was the thickest penis?

Small was the smallest erect penis?

Saggy was the saggiest sack?

# 102

What does it mean to you if a woman "spits or swallows" while giving head?

# Sheer Silk

*Breasts and nipples adore attention. Caress them through silk. Enjoy the ultra smooth texture. Delicately stroke each entire breast with your fingers. Circle her nipples and feel them stiffen with desire. Using your palms, lightly rub the tender buds with a circular motion. Notice the subtle features of her nipples as they react to your sensual touch.*

# 103

What article of clothing would you most like me to wear or keep on during sex?

# 104

What types of sexy clothing or lingerie gets you aroused? What color and style of sexy underwear do you prefer and why?

# 105

How do you feel about cross dressing and to what extent would you go to "transform" either or both of us into the opposite sex for role playing?

# 106

Do you find the smell of my worn clothing arousing? What types of clothing?

# 107

What is your favorite role playing character or situation either in fantasy or one you've acted out?

# 108

Have you ever shopped for sexy items online? How do you feel about browsing the internet for sex toys or lingerie together?

# 109

If you could magically live the part as one of the characters in any movie scene but change the events for your sexual pleasure, what movie, character and scene would you want to experience?

# 110

If you were to fantasize or role play a sexy scenario involving one or both of us being a celebrity, who and what would be the scenario when:

I am the celebrity?
You are the celebrity?
We are both celebrities?

# Clowning Around

*Humor is very important in a relationship. Sex should be fun as well as intimate and loving. Many women claim that the most attractive aspect of their partner is their sense of humor. A bit of humor may stimulate your mind and distract it from your physical arousal. Used at the right moment, you can prolong the loving and enjoy it even more.*

# 111

What is the most hilarious or embarrassing thing that has ever happened while you were having sex?

# 112

What kinds of unusual things do you find erotic and get turned on by?

# 113

What is the best dirty joke that you can remember? What kinds of dirty jokes do you like? If you were to come up with more dirty jokes for us to enjoy together, where would you find them?

# 114

What's the worst thing you've done with a used condom?

# 115

What is the most unusual or outrageous type of erotic outfit that you'd like to wear to fulfill a fantasy or express a secret desire?

# 116

Have you ever farted while a lover was going down on you? How would you react if I farted while you were going down on me?

# 117

What ingredients went into the messiest sex you've ever had? How would you like to get even dirtier together?

# 118

Rather than filming ourselves having sex, how would you feel about making a video of an erotic puppet show together? What kind of naughty scenario would you want to perform? What kind of props would you want to include in the show?

# Fancy Feast

*Invite your lover to savor your oral delicacies prepared in elegant style. Visual appeal enhances the sensuality and stimulates erotic hunger. Use stockings, high heels, garter belts, crotch-less panties or any other type of lingerie to dress up your special treat. While your lover eagerly laps up your fancy feast, the feline in you will be clawing at the floor and purring with pleasure.*

# 119

What color and style of lingerie do you prefer and why? Do you prefer to remove the lingerie before having sex or to keep it on?

# 120

Have you ever been to a fantasy or erotic role playing costume party? What costumes would you choose for us if we were to go to one? Is this the same type of role play costume you would like to wear in the bedroom or would you dress in one even more erotic?

# 121

What makes receiving oral sex feel great? What takes oral sex from being good to being fantastic?

# 122

What types of clothing do I wear that makes you think of having sex? What color of clothing do you think is most attractive?

# 123

In what situation and with what type of clothing would you like to enjoy sex fully dressed?

# 124

Have you ever experimented with cross dressing? Would you cross-dress for a role playing scenario?

# 125

What color of nail polish do you find sexy on a woman? How do you feel about playful scratching during foreplay or while having sex?

# 126

If we could paint our bodies each one color before a night of wild sex, what colors would you choose for us?

# Oral Offer

*In a public setting, casually interject an oral offer that will have him thinking of you for the rest of the night. Smiling sweetly, tell him specifically how you are going to suck his cock. Promise to swallow.*

## 127

In what areas of your body other than your genitals do you enjoy oral pleasuring?

## 128

How and when would you like me to talk dirty to you? How dirty is dirty?

## 129

How many different words, terms or names can you think of for:

| | |
|---|---|
| Female privates? | Female breasts? |
| Male privates? | Buttocks? |
| Anus? | Anal Sex? |
| Masturbation? | Intercourse? |
| Cunnilingus? | Fellatio? |

## 130

What words do you prefer to use for male and female sexy bits? What pet names would you like to call our genitals?

# 131

If I was to lick the alphabet or letters of sexy words on different parts of your body, where would you most like this tasty tongue twister technique tried? On which erogenous zone do you think you could determine what I was spelling out?

# 132

If you were to write me a sex coupon to be redeemed sometime later this week, what would it involve? What kind of sex coupon would you like me to write for you?

# 133

Have you ever played any erotic truth or dare games? What's the wildest sex dare you can think of? What's the wildest truth question you can think of?

# 134

Have you ever used a dildo or vibrator with a lover? In what ways?

# Big Talker

*Although men are visual creatures, they find phone sex extremely arousing if done right. Stimulate mental pictures in specific, graphic detail. Describe how big and hard he is and how wet and horny you are. Gasp, pant, moan, sigh. Beg for it as you tease him with fantasies that you may or may not want in reality. Tell juicy stories of masturbation, other women, anal sex, bondage and other taboo topics.*

# 135

In what ways do you think we can use our cell phones to get each other both excited and ready for hot sex together?

# 136

What would your penis/pussy say if it could talk:

Only to my pussy/penis?
Only to me without you knowing?
Aloud to you while I secretly listened?
As a hand puppet for a sex ed show?

# 137

In what ways do you think we can use hot erotic talk to get each other more excited? What kinds of slang or swear words do you feel are okay for dirty talk during our sex play? What dirty words would you prefer not to hear?

# 138

What length and thickness do you feel would make the best sized penis? What size and shape of penis do you consider most attractive?

# 139

What is the naughtiest thing you can think of to whisper in my ear right now?

# 140

What was the farthest you have ever shot your load or squirted during a G-spot orgasm? How far do you think you can get if we tried right now?

# 141

What made up super hero name would you give for your erotic persona?

# 142

If we were both porn actors, what would be our individual traits or special sex acts that would make us stars?

# Delightful Devices

*Vibrators and dildos come in all shapes, sizes and textures. Sex toys are great for both sexes alone or with a partner. Shake up your world and experience a battery powered orgasm tonight.*

## 143

Other than being ever hard and ready, in what ways do you think a dildo is better than a real penis?

## 144

What is the first thing that comes to your mind when you hear "sex toys"? Do you normally think of sex toys as pleasuring aids for women, men or couples?

## 145

If you were to design the ultimate sex toy for either women, men or couples, how would it look and what features would it have?

## 146

What sex toys for guys would you like to use in our sex play?

# 147

What are your favorite sex toys for:
    Masturbation?
    Sex play together?

# 148

Have you ever used sex toys:
    In the shower or bath?
    While traveling in a vehicle?
    With your clothes on?
    While talking on the phone?
    To finish the job after sex?

# 149

What's the weirdest looking sex toy you've ever seen or used? What shapes and sizes of vibrators and dildos do you own?

# 150

What's your favorite style and color of dildo or vibrator? If you could customize the design of your favorite sex toy, what colors would you use?

# Passion Guide

*Enlist the guidance of your lover to explore new sexual territory together. Have them select a special activity they would like to experience fully and completely. Ask them to detail every intimate desire that would improve their passion and pleasure. Discover the path to their ecstasy and you will be rewarded. Communication is the key. Talking before, during and after is absolutely essential.*

# 151

If you could telepathically connect with anyone while they were having sex and experience all their sensations, who would you want to link up with and why?

# 152

What tips do you think we could learn from lesbians to improve our love making? What tips do you think we could learn from gay men?

# 153

When and how did you first learn about sex?

# 154

What benefits do you think we can get from watching porn together?

# 155

How do you feel about your first sexual experiences? If you could change one thing about them, what would you alter and why?

# 156

At what age did you first see an adult movie with sex? How explicit was it and what feelings do you remember having?

# 157

What's the funniest tip you have ever heard or seen in a sex advice article? What are the best and worst tips you've come across from a sex expert?

# 158

If you had to give verbal instructions to someone about to make love for the first time, what would you say to help them perform:

> Great foreplay?
> A blow job?
> Cunnilingus?
> G-spot stimulation?
> Satisfying intercourse?

## Close Embrace

*The classic missionary position is excellent for maintaining a close embrace. No matter how intense your sex play has become, continue kissing and fondling each other with ever increasing passion. By wrapping her legs around him and pulling him closer, she can encourage more stimulation of her clitoris and pace his thrusts for mutual satisfaction.*

# 159

Which sex positions do you find most:
Comfortable?          Intimate?
Stimulating?          Thrilling?

# 160

How many different Kama Sutra sex positions do you think you have done? How many can you name?

# 161

Have you ever shaved another person's private parts? What style of pubic hair do you prefer?

# 162

Do you enjoy or think you would enjoy the feel of hard cold glass or steel dildos?

# 163

What color paint would you want to use to make artistic body prints?

# 164

Do you prefer playing with:
Hard or soft dildos?
Hard or soft vibrators?
Insertable or clitoral vibrators?
Realistic penis or non-penis shaped dildos?

# 165

Do you like something in your vagina while your clitoris is stimulated to orgasm either orally, manually or with a vibrator?

# 166

Do you like balls attached to your dildos for realism or do you prefer some other type of grip?

# 167

Would you ever consider swapping partners for a night of hot sex? Would it be someone we know or would it need to be with strangers?

# Carried Away

*Bring each other to a fevered state of arousal kissing and fondling. When you are overwhelmed with passionate desire that requires urgent relief, throw caution to the wind and carry her away to ecstasy. Standing, he lifts her up onto his cock as she wraps her legs and arms around him. Fuel your stamina with wild lust.*

# 168

Have you ever done a 69 position standing or sitting up? Would you like to try doing it together?

# 169

Have you ever had sex:
> Without any kissing?
> Without taking any clothing off?
> Before reaching the bedroom?
> Loudly so other people could hear?
> With other people watching?

# 170

In which situation would you most likely offer me a quickie when you're feeling extra naughty?
> A: Just before I'm about to leave for work
> B: Shortly before we're expecting visitors

# 171

Will you still have sex even if it's that time of month? How would you feel about role playing a "deflowering" scenario during this time?

# 172

While working out together at a gym, you discover we're all alone and you're feeling naughty. Where would you rather have sex?

    A:  On any convenient exercise equipment
    B:  In the shower, sauna or tanning booth

# 173

In what ways can you imagine having sex at work? If you've ever had sex at work what was it like for you? Would you like to have sex at work with me?

# 174

What's the most daring sexual thing you have or would like to do in a public location like a store, bar, restaurant or movie theatre?

# Bathing and Bonding

*Soaking together in a warm bath of aromatic oils provides an opportunity for delicious skin-to-skin contact. Gently massage and stroke each other in a silent expression of love. These intimate moments help keep your sensuality alive and form the foundation for a deeply satisfying sexual relationship.*

# 175

To enhance our sexual potential, how would you feel about taking a course together in:

Yoga?              Ballroom dance?
Massage?           Tantric sex?

# 176

Other than in the bedroom, what location in our home is your favorite place to have sex?

# 177

What do you feel are the keys to a long lasting, monogamous relationship?

# 178

How can we arrange our day so we have lots of time to enjoy more foreplay together?

# 179

In what ways do you feel we can better communicate our desires?

# 180

How long do you think we could have intercourse without any thrusting or hip movement? Do you think either of us could reach an orgasm using only our PC muscles?

# 181

Do you feel I read your body language and get your signals right most of the time? Do you feel I know when you want sex to be sensual or more passionately intense?

# 182

How can we make sure we remain happily faithful and committed to each other in a long term relationship?

# Wicked Hand Job

*When manually stimulating your lover, give them pleasure from both hands. Let them sample a forbidden sensual delight. As you stroke their genitals, tickle and massage their ass. Add some lubricant and, when they are close to climax, gently ease a finger into their anus. Explore and stimulate each other's darker desires.*

# 183

Have you ever been anally pleasured with a finger, butt plug or anal dildo while:

Receiving or performing a hand job?
Receiving or performing oral sex?
Having intercourse?

# 184

If you could use only one hand to pleasure me, what kinds of things would you do?

# 185

Have you ever given or received a "foot job"? Would you like to try it together?

# 186

How do you feel about facials? What about ejaculation on other body parts?

# 187

What erotic role playing or fantasy scenarios can you imagine that involve getting a spanking for being naughty? Have you ever enjoyed sex play that involved spanking?

# 188

Either alone or with a partner, have you every used or would you like to try using:

Butt plugs?          Anal dildos?
Anal beads?          Anal probes?

# 189

Have you ever used a vibrator:

To masturbate at work?
And worn out fresh batteries in one session?
So much it burnt out or started to smoke?
In a public place with people around?
Wirelessly controlled by someone else?

# 190

Using a dildo or fake pussy, have you ever practiced or demonstrated:

Different hand job techniques?
How to perform oral sex?
How to put on a condom?
Using your mouth to put on a condom?

# Bound to Please

*Bondage plays a part in many types of fantasies. With a trusted, loving partner, it can be a very thrilling experience. Either as the submissive or dominant, a little restraint can help you both explore some intensely emotional aspects of your mind. These emotions can heighten the physical sensations of your love play.*

## 191

How do you feel about experimenting with bondage? If I was tied up, what kinds of kinky things can you imagine doing with me?

## 192

What forms of BDSM play have you heard of and how do you feel about them? Are there any BDSM sex play ideas you would like to try?

## 193

If we were to play out a bondage fantasy scenario, how would you feel about role playing a:

Mad scientist doing sexual experiments?
Captured spy being interrogated?
Slave disciplined by a deviant owner?
Sorcerer performing a dark ritual?
Cruel dungeon master doing his "job"?

# 194

What kinds of bondage devices or contraptions can you imagine using as part of our sex play? Which ones would you like to try and how would we use them?

# 195

What kinds of sex play activities, role play scenarios or erotic story ideas can you think of involving bondage?

# 196

What kinds of BDSM sex toys, devices or accessories do you own or would like to own? When playing with BDSM sex toys, do you prefer to be the dominant or submissive player?

# 197

If we were to experiment with bondage or SM play, what safe word would you like to use to stop our sex play if it gets too intense?

# Sinful Under Satin

*Indulge your temptation for satin sheets. The smooth, slippery surface of satin creates sensual delights that are absolutely sinful. Your supple bodies will slither and slide into new sexual positions with ease. Sparingly use your satin sheets as a seductive surprise.*

## 198

What color and type of bedsheets or covering do you find most:

Romantic?         Sensual?
Erotic?           Sexy?

## 199

What kinds of sex play activities make you feel:

A deep intimate and loving connection?
A sense of naughty excitement?
Delightfully submissive?
Sexually confident and in control?
Nasty, dirty and wickedly playful?

## 200

What items should every couple have in their bedroom for great sex?

## 201

What do you fantasize about while masturbating with a dildo?

# 202

When watching porn, what types of sex acts do you find most erotic or sexually arousing?

# 203

As a great reason to go to sleep naked, which erotic night time activity would you most enjoy?

    A: Having your way with me while I was still asleep or semi awake

    B: Having me stimulating your wet dreams with my mouth and fingers

# 204

What size of dildo or insertable vibrator do you most like to play with?

# 205

Would you rather have me roleplay as a sexy yet innocent angel or a hot and naughty devil? What kind of erotic scenario or fantasy involving an angel or devil would turn you on?

# Over The Edge

*During the heat of passion, you may drive each other to the point of almost toppling out of bed. The sense of wild abandon heightens your erotic thrill. Why leave it to chance. Position yourselves over the edge of your bed and feel the exhilarating rush as you build toward an intense orgasm. Hold on tight for a fun ride Over the Edge.*

# 206

What new or rarely used types of sex positions would you like to experiment with?

# 207

What is the wildest location or situation that you have ever had sex? What is the wildest, craziest location you can think of to make love?

# 208

What kinds of different sex positions or activities do you think we can perform using:

A sturdy chair?
A blowup exercise ball?
Lots of pillows or cushions?
A hammock?
A pool table?

# 209

What is the most shocking type of pornographic scene you can think of that would be erotically thrilling to watch even if it's something you wouldn't want to do yourself?

# 210

When using a dildo for sex play either solo or with a partner, have you ever:

Licked or sucked on it?
Put a condom on it?
Attached it to something for hands free play?
Used more than one at the same time?

# 211

Have you ever had or would you like to have sex in:

An elevator?          A restroom?
A parking lot?        A back alley?
A seedy motel?        A Stairwell?

# 212

What kinds of activities do you consider to be kinky? What are some kinky activities you would like to try and what are off limits for you?

# Slow & Sensual Tease

*Dress seductively in silky lingerie and stockings. With your lover waiting and watching on the bed, tease them as you titillate yourself. Coyly use your eyes and lips to seduce them with unspoken desire. Massage your breasts and stroke your nipples until they stiffen. Feel naughty as you lick your finger tips and slip them into your panties. Slowly masturbate for them until they yearn for your tantalizing touch.*

# 213

Have you ever masturbated to visually arouse a lover? Have you ever played with yourself to show a lover how you like it?

# 214

Have you ever secretly watched someone masturbate? Do you find it more erotic and arousing watching a woman or man masturbate? Do you get turned on by watching me play with myself?

# 215

Do you have:

A mini-vibe for clitoral stimulation?
An insertable vibrator for penetration?
A g-spot vibrator or dildo?
A glass or steel dildo?
A double ended dildo?

# 216

What types of lingerie do you find most:
Sexually exciting?
Sensually appealing?
Romantic?

# 217

If someone wanted to pay to watch us having sex, what price and conditions would you want before agreeing? How much would you want to have it filmed as a hard core porn video?

# 218

What is the most erotic movie scene you have ever watched? What hot and sexy scene would you most like to re-enact together?

# 219

If you were to secretly discover someone in a sexy situation, which would you find more erotic and what would you like to see them doing?
A: Someone masturbating
B: A couple making love

# Taste Sensations

*Gather up a few oral treats (chocolate sauce, liquors, yogurt, honey, caramel, whip cream, etc.). Dribble your goodies on sensitive areas of your lover then lick them clean.*

## 220

What flavor or scent of massage oil do you find the most arousing? What kinds of stimulating lubricants, oils or creams would you like to try?

## 221

Do you like the way I taste when performing oral sex? What type of flavored lube would make it even tastier?

## 222

What kinds of aphrodisiacs have you heard or read about? Which ones have you tried and are there any that work for you?

## 223

If you were to create a cocktail drink that represents how I taste (or would like me to taste) when you go down on me, what ingredients would you include and what would you call it?

# 224

If orgasms created a taste or smell sensation, what type of flavor or scent would you want for your climax?

# 225

What is the most intimate fun you have ever had with food? What kinds of food or edible substances would you like to use in our sex play?

# 226

Have you ever used hot sauce to spice up your sex life? What's the strangest edible substance you have ever used in your sex play?

# 227

What creatively sensual activities can you imagine doing to each other with:

| | |
|---|---|
| Chocolate? | Whipped cream? |
| Pieces of mango? | Sweet liquor? |
| Honey or syrup? | Ice or popsicles? |
| String liquorice? | Black balls? |
| Icing sugar? | Jello or pudding? |

# Joy Riding

*When the woman takes control of her lover's stick shift, get ready for more than a pleasure ride. He lies on his back and she straddles him on her knees. In this female superior position, she controls the twists and turns as well as the speed. He should try to relax as she grinds her gears with his on a wild ride to ecstasy.*

# 228

What color and style of car or truck would you most like to have sex in? What kinds of frisky activities have you ever performed in or on a car?

# 229

Do you travel with sex toys? Do you carry a mini-vibe with you? Have you ever had your luggage inspected with sex toys in it? What happened and how did you feel?

# 230

What is the fastest time you can remember that:

A partner orgasmed when having sex?
You orgasmed when having sex?
A lover made you come with oral sex?
You made someone come with oral sex?
You made yourself orgasm masturbating?

# 231

What new sex position or activity have you imagined us doing together?

# 232

What would you include in a picnic basket for a romantic outing and where would we go?

# 233

If we were to go on a sexy shopping spree together, what would you most like to get and which stores would you want to visit?

# 234

In what way would you most like to add the "thrill of getting caught" to our sex play to make it even more exciting?

# 235

What is the kinkiest public place you have ever had sex? Where and how would you most like to have sex in a semi-public location?

# Simple Satisfaction

*The basic missionary position is a very comfortable way to make love gently and sensuously. You are able to make eye contact, kiss and caress each other while maintaining almost full body contact.*

## 236

What is your favorite position for:
Making love?
Having wild sex?
Having a quickie?

## 237

What defines the difference between foreplay, sex play and after play?

## 238

How much foreplay do you desire on average before the main event? What's your signal that you're ready for more?

## 239

If we were to role play as strangers looking for anonymous sex, how many different scenarios can you think of? What kind of scenario would turn you on the most?

# 240

What do you most enjoy about:
> Performing oral sex?
> Receiving oral sex?
> Performing a hand job?
> Receiving a hand job?

# 241

How many times do you masturbate on average per week? When and where do you prefer to masturbate?

# 242

Of all the places you have ever had sex outside the bedroom, where would you say was the:

| | |
|---|---|
| Best? | Worst? |
| Dirtiest? | Kinkiest? |
| Most thrilling? | Tightest? |
| Most dangerous? | Dumbest? |

# 243

What do you think is the sexiest sport or competition to either play or watch?

# Innocence Lost

*Shock and amaze your lover and yourself. Do something completely unexpected. Let your imagination go wild and explore the limitless erotic possibilities available to thrill and excite your lover. Become outrageously wicked even if just for a moment. Lose your innocence again and again.*

# 244

What is the most forbidden or taboo sexual activity you can imagine doing together?

# 245

Have you ever lost a:
  Condom inside?
  Plaything up the bum?

# 246

What is the kinkiest type of foreplay activity that:
  First comes to mind right now?
  You can think of anyone ever doing?
  You have ever experienced?
  You have ever performed?
  You would like to try?

# 247

Have you ever masturbated using a piece of fruit or a vegetable like carrots, cucumbers or zucchini?

# 248

Of all the types of sex play activities you can think of or have experienced:

> What is the most nasty or dirty?
> What is the most wild or crazy?
> What is the most naughty or forbidden?

# 249

Do you know what the sexual term:

> ATM stands for?
> "Fisting" involves?
> "Figging" involves?
> "Rimming" involves?
> "Splooshing" involves?
> "Pony Play" involves?

# 250

What's the strangest thing you have ever pleasured yourself with? At what age did you first use a sex toy?

# 251

Have you ever:

> Used a strap-on with a partner?
> Used a double penetration dildo?
> Masturbated with a butt plug or anal dildo?
> Used a simulated tongue device?
> Caused a squirting orgasm with a G-spot vibrator or dildo?

## Passion for Play

*Stimulate intense passionate desire with a teasing sequence of erotic play. Start by telling your lover how desirable they are. Arouse interest then wait. Detail the intensity of your lust and how you want to ravish them. Then wait. Kiss and fondle your lover. Stimulate then stop. Progressively build the erotic excitement until neither one of you can resist each other.*

# 252

What kinds of erotic games have you played? What kinds of sexy games would you like to play either together or with close friends?

# 253

What was the best adult or couples game that you have ever played and what did you like about it?

# 254

While naked together with a lover, have you ever:

Had a pillow fight?
Had a water gun fight?
Wrestled covered in oil?
Run around in the snow?
Played on a swing set?
Gazed at the night sky?

# 255

What was the first sex game you've ever played? If you were to come up with a sex game for us to play, what would it involve and how would we play it?

# 256

How would you change the rules of a regular game we've played together to make it into a hot sex game? When would you like to play it with me?

# 257

Think of any game show on TV. How would you imagine playing an erotic version of it and what would be some of the prizes?

# 258

Have you ever played any strip games like strip poker with a group of people? Who else would you want to invite if we were to play a stripping game with other people?

## Sightless Sensations

*Blindfold your lover to heighten their other senses. Without speaking, use anticipation and suspense to build arousal as you tantalize their senses with tastes, textures and toys.*

## 259

Have you ever been tied up, blindfolded and sensually teased? What would you do to me if you had me tied up and blindfolded?

## 260

To enhance our foreplay with new stimulating sensations, what kind and how would you like to use:

A sex toy for women?
A sex toy for men?
A sex toy for couples?
An anal sex toy?
A kinky or fetish accessory?

## 261

Is there a certain kind of perfume or cologne that gets you in the mood?

## 262

What foods or smells get you turned on or thinking about having sex?

# 263

How much and what types of kissing do you enjoy? Do we kiss enough before, during or after sex?

# 264

While enjoying a blow job, have you or your partner ever enhanced the sensation by:

Using ice cubes and hot tea?
Sucking on black ball candies?
Sucking on a strong mint?
Popping in a few small marshmallows?
Deep throating?

# 265

Do you prefer realistic penis shaped dildos and vibrators or other types of designs?

# 266

Do you like to use a vibrator to stimulate other parts of the body besides the pussy/clitoris?

# Creative Control

*Uninhibited, spontaneous sexual activities can be exhilarating, but exercising a little creative control has its own rewards. Spend some time alone or together to plan the details of an amazing sexual adventure. Consider it advanced foreplay.*

## 267

If budget was not a consideration and you had access to a full production crew, what type of erotic movie would you want to make and what role would you play in it?

## 268

If you were going to throw an erotically themed party, what theme would you choose and what kinds of things or activities would be included?

## 269

If we were to create a piece of erotic art together using our naked bodies, which style of artwork would you prefer?

A: Apply paint to our bodies and make an impression on canvas

B: Create a plaster cast of parts of our bodies to make a statue

# 270

If you were to make an erotic accessory to enjoy either alone or together, what kinds of things would you consider making?

# 271

Imagine that you had a team of scientists and engineers that could build anything you desired using advanced technologies most people could only dream about. What features and capabilities would you want in:

    The ultimate sex robot?
    The ultimate sex toy?
    A body enhancement?
    A special sex pill?
    A fantasy simulator?

# 272

How would you feel about role playing as an erotic photographer or model? If we were to make an erotic slide show or photo album of us using digital pictures, what types of images would you want taken of:

    You?
    Me?
    Us?

# Double Entry

*Many women fantasize about being completely filled up. Whether you have a spare cock on hand or not, you can fulfill the fantasy with a penis double. A dildo or vibrator are quick substitutes when you need to make a double entry. Let her decide if you get to pleasure her anally or vaginally.*

# 273

Have you tried double or triple penetration with multiple guys involved at the same time? How would you feel about doing it again or simulating it using a dildo or insertable vibrator?

# 274

Have you ever used a double dildo together with a lover for mutual anal pleasure? How do you feel about trying it together?

# 275

Have you ever made a mess on the bed while having anal sex? Have you ever used an enema before anal intercourse?

# 276

What's the kinkiest sex toy you have ever tried, seen or wished for?

# 277

What kinds of fetishes have you heard about that arouse your interest? If you had a sexual fetish, what would you say it involved?

# 278

What is the wildest sexual fetish you can think of that you might like to explore together? What kinds of fetish play do you think would get you excited?

# 279

What do you think is the most taboo sexual desire that you've satisfied or been tempted to try?

# 280

What are the most intriguing types of sex techniques, positions or activities you've seen in porn movies that you would like to experiment with?

# Aural Sex

*Many people have a preference for aural stimulation. A sensual voice can arouse fantasies and heighten desire. The art of erotic talk is a talent that can be learned and perfected with practice. Your voice can convey sensuality and lust. Single words whispered at the right moment can trigger an orgasm. Call your lover and explore your aural erogenous zones.*

## 281

Have you ever listened to:
> A porn movie without watching the video?
> An erotic audio story or guided fantasy?
> A sexual hypnosis or self improvement CD?
> An audio recording of your lovemaking?
> Someone read you an erotic story or letter?

## 282

Think of a classic fairy tale or children's story. How would you retell this story as a naughty adult fantasy?

## 283

What specific words or sounds enhance your passion and desire for sex? What kinds of different background sounds have you tried making love to?

# 284

Besides your name, what are the sexiest things I could say to you during sex?

# 285

What words or phrases do you use or associate with:

Feeling sexually aroused?
Romantic lovemaking?
Wild, passionate sex?
Having an orgasm?

# 286

In how many creative ways can you think of using any form of music to enhance our sex play?

# 287

What different types of music have you tried making love to? If you were to pick a style of music we don't normally listen to and have sex with it playing, what kind would you want to try?

# Different Strokes

*While masturbating and during intercourse, many people tend to use the same technique. To learn about your arousal response, help maintain a longer erection and intensify your orgasm, experiment with different strokes. When you are about to climax, switch strokes. Vary the pressure, speed, direction, position, etc. to alter the sensation. You could even change fantasies. Learn to use multiple techniques in various combinations to pleasure yourself and your lover.*

## 288

What techniques do you use to masturbate? How long does it take you to stimulate yourself to orgasm?

## 289

Have you ever used body paints or markers for fun sex play? What kind of design can you imagine painting or drawing on my body?

## 290

What are your favorite online sex sites and what do you like about them? How would you feel about browsing the internet for sexy content together?

# 291

What kinds of kinky sex play accessories do you think you could find in the kitchen? What would you do with them?

# 292

What kinds of sex toys would you purchase for me:

To masturbate with?
To stimulate you?
To use together or on each other?

# 293

Have you ever made or used a sex machine? Have you ever seen any sex machines in action online or in porn and if so which one was the most fascinating?

# 294

What television shows do you feel have the most sexually inspiring characters or scenes?

# Lovely in Lace

*Any color and style of lingerie looks lovely on a woman. Lace, satin and silk enables her to express all of her sultry desires. Sexy clothing can alter her mood instantly while stimulating both your fantasies. Acutely aware of her alluring powers, she will transform into a sex goddess. Leave lights and lingerie on while making love.*

# 295

Have you ever specifically dressed up just before having sex? Have you ever dressed in an outfit so that your lover could rip and tear it off of you?

# 296

Which situation would you find most seductive and arousing?

- A: Me performing an erotic strip tease before having sex naked
- B: Me wearing a sexy outfit and keeping it on while having sex

# 297

What one part of my body do you find most:

Attractive?          Arousing?
Touchable?          Kissable?
Lickable?            Suckable?

# 298

What type of male profession do you feel has the most erotic or attractive uniforms? What type of female profession do you feel has the hottest looking style of dress? If we were to role play a scenario involving one of these occupations, which one would you want to try?

# 299

What is the most daring outfit or lack of clothing you've worn or would like to wear out in public? How does it make you feel?

# 300

What style and color of leather or latex outfit would you like to see either of us wear?

# 301

Have you ever used or would you like to try using:
Nipple clamps?
Clit clips?
Erotic body jewelry?

# Mutual Masturbation

*In new and long term relationships, an evening of mutual masturbation will help you learn about each other while enhancing your intimacy. Play some soft music to set the mood. While stroking yourself, describe what you are doing and how it feels. Demonstrate your techniques. Close your eyes and fantasize if you desire. Have your lover kiss and caress you to enhance the experience.*

# 302

How do you feel about having me watch as you masturbate?

# 303

What do you feel are the benefits of masturbation?

# 304

Do you masturbate with sex toys? Do you ever masturbate without using a sex toy? How are your orgasms different when using a sex toy and when you don't?

# 305

Do you masturbate to porn or use erotica to get you aroused before switching to your own fantasies?

# 306

Imagine we mentally switch bodies every time we have sex and switch back when we both have an orgasm. We think the same but experience sex with this new body. How would this affect your desire to:

Try mutual masturbation?
Receive oral sex?
Perform oral sex?
Prefer "spit or swallow"?
Have anal sex?
Try new foreplay ideas?
Try new sex positions?
Role play certain fantasies?
Be more kinky together?

# 307

How would you react if I made you a video of me masturbating? What kinds of things would you like to see me doing in the video? What type of camera angle or shot would you prefer?

# 308

Have you ever used a mirror to watch yourself having sex or masturbating? Would you like to try using a mirror together?

# Bedtime Story

*A little bedtime reading can provide the inspiration for some truly great sex. Fire up your fantasies with erotic fiction or explicit pictorials. Read a favorite story to your lover involving a personal fantasy to gauge their reaction. Erotic stories can provide ideas for new activities, scenarios or exotic role playing opportunities.*

## 309

What are some books you've read that most inspired your erotic imagination? What type of reading material turns you on the most?

## 310

In what ways can you imagine turning each other on while we're apart?

## 311

What kinds of erotica do you enjoy for self pleasure or masturbation?

## 312

How would you feel about joining an online sex chat or adult role playing forum together?

# 313

What is the weirdest sexual activity you have every heard, read, seen or thought about?

# 314

What is the most intriguing sexual fantasy your have ever heard or read about?

# 315

What erotic fantasies, sexy stories or role playing scenarios can you think of that would fit the title:

It's Just Business?
First Encounter?
Bound to Please?
It Came In The Night?
Innocence Lost?
Prize Possession?
It's All Arranged?
Caught by Surprise?
Private Ceremony?
Barely Legal?
Desperate Measures?
Professional Service?
Magic Powers?
Winner Takes All?
Service With a Smile?
Up Against the Wall?
On Display?
Exchange of Power?

# Private Dancer

*A strip tease is visually erotic. The key to a great strip tease is seductive eye contact. Wear lots of easily removed clothing and play some specially selected mood music. Slowly remove each piece of clothing while wiggling and swaying provocatively. Tease with a slow simulation of your sexual desires. Build anticipation for the physical pleasures to come.*

## 316

Have you ever performed a strip tease, lap dance or belly dance? Would you ever take a course or watch a DVD on how to perform an erotic dance?

## 317

What types of visual stimulation gets you excited?

## 318

Have you ever:

Been to a live sex show?
Gone streaking?
Stripped in public?
Been to a nudist resort?

## 319

Would you consider yourself more of an exhibitionist or voyeur and why?

# 320

Have you ever slow danced naked before making love? What song would you like to try this with?

# 321

Under what conditions or circumstances would you have sex for money? How much would you charge?

# 322

What color and style of high heels do you think are sexy? How do you feel about wearing high heels and stockings in bed while having sex?

# 323

What type of dance do you feel is the most erotic to either watch or perform? How would you feel about learning this type of dance together so we can perform it naked with each other?

# Sensual Bliss

*During intercourse, close your eyes and experience the physical expression of each other's love. Consciously slow every movement. Allow your emotions to swirl together with the feelings of sensual intimacy you're sharing. Your mutual love for each other will amplify even simple pleasures. Each stimulus will contribute to the overwhelming joy of complete sensual bliss.*

# 324

What other types of stimulation do you need during intercourse to increase your ability to orgasm?

# 325

What is the hottest thing I could whisper in your ear just before you orgasm?

# 326

On average how long do you feel foreplay should last? Do you feel we are having enough foreplay before sex?

# 327

Have you every used or would you like to try using a dildo made of:

| | |
|---|---|
| Ice? | Glass? |
| Steel? | Marble? |

# 328

Do you prefer to keep your eyes open or closed while kissing or having sex? Have you ever looked into a lover's eyes as you or they were having an orgasm?

# 329

Imagine that both of us gained the power to transform into the opposite sex and back again any time we desired.

> In what ways would you ever want to use this power either alone or together?
> When you transform, what physical features would you give yourself?
> Would you want to experiment with gay or lesbian sex together?
> If we both switched, what types of foreplay would you like to experience?
> What types of sexual activities would you most want to try?

# 330

If orgasms created flashes of color in your mind, what colors would you see?

# 331

Have you ever fallen asleep while being pleasured in any way?

# Arousing Atmosphere

*Creatively engage all five senses for the ultimate in sensual pleasure. Light candles to create an erotic and mysterious atmosphere. Burn fragrant oils or incense to sooth or stimulate. Use flavored oils to whet the appetite. Play music to set the mood. Then tantalize with your touch.*

# 332

How can I best set the mood for a night of romantic love making?

# 333

What is the key factor that affects your desire to have sex? What types of things can I do that would increase your desire to have even more sex?

# 334

What types of music do you find:
Most romantic?
Most sexually arousing?
Best for making love?

# 335

What color and type of lighting in the bedroom do you think is the most:

Romantic?     Sexy?
Erotic?       Exciting?

# 336

What ingredients would be involved in your recipe for the ultimate night of hot sex?

# 337

On what days and times of day do you most feel like:

Enjoying more sensual foreplay?
Getting frisky and playful?
Having a quickie?
Making love?
Masturbating?

# 338

What do you like to do to get ready for a great session of:

Romantic intimacy?
Sex together?
Self pleasuring?

# 339

If you were designing a secret love den, adult play room or sex dungeon for the two of us, how would it look and what would you include in it? Try to describe it in as much detail as you can (style, color, toys, accessories, furniture, etc.).

# Reclined, Relaxed, Ready

*Sitting comfortably on a chair with her lover kneeling before her, she closes her eyes and relaxes in anticipation. Sensual kisses and licks tingle the skin on her inner thighs. As the arousal builds, she opens for the warm tickle of a soft rhythmic tongue. Feathery light tongue swirls and hot breaths on her clitoris bring shudders of sheer delight.*

## 340

Have you ever received oral sex while blindfolded?

## 341

Have you ever experienced a blended g-spot and cunnilingus orgasm? Including female ejaculation?

## 342

If I could hypnotize you and make you believe my penis/clitoris tasted like a candy when you performed oral sex, what flavor would you prefer?

## 343

What kinds of pornography have you seen and which types do you like best?

# 344

How much and what kinds of foreplay do you feel is best before:

Sexual intercourse?
Anal intercourse?
Oral sex?

# 345

What types of foreplay would you like more of?

# 346

Suppose a machine was invented that could somehow stimulate a highly detailed, realistic, memorable and intense "wet dream" involving any type of sexual fantasy. What type of fantasy would you most like to experience?

# 347

What tips can you tell me for improving how I perform oral sex for you?

# Uniquely Beautiful

*Every penis is different in size, shape, coloring, taste and texture. Depending upon his arousal level, his penis will also have differences from one erection to another. A woman's labia and vagina are also unique to her alone. Explore each other's intimate parts to identify all their unique characteristics throughout all the various stages of arousal.*

## 348

Have you ever created a penis or pussy mold to make a silicone replica? How would you feel about making a matching set of our sexy bits?

## 349

What do you feel are the most attractive features of:

Women?
Men?

## 350

Do you prefer a penis with foreskin or would you rather have it circumcised? Do you prefer a penis that grows as it becomes erect or one that stays about the same size even when flaccid?

# 351

If we were to get matching erotic tattoos, what designs would you want for each of us and where would you want them located on our bodies?

# 352

If we were to each get an erotic body piercing together, what type of body jewelry would you want for each of us and where would you want the piercings to be on our bodies?

# 353

What aspects do you find most erotic in people of:

The opposite sex?
The same sex?
A different race or culture?

# 354

How do you feel about taking a life drawing or painting course together so we can learn how to create our own private erotic art of each other?

# Monumental Mating

*Strive to make each of your love making sessions exceptionally great. But every now and then, focus on pleasuring each other totally. Concentrate on every detail. Add just the right amount of love and fantasy to create enduring and memorable moments of intimacy that you can share for eternity.*

# 355

If we had started a sexual scrapbook or memory box when we first got together, what kinds of things would you have put in it?

# 356

Have you ever had or would you like to have sex:

> In a tree house?
> In a tent?
> In a log cabin?
> By an open fire?
> Outside under the stars?

# 357

What is the largest dildo you have ever inserted:

> Orally?
> Vaginally?
> Anally?

# 358

What's the most number of orgasms you remember having in one session of sex?

# 359

If we were to create a private erotic tradition for the two of us on special occasions, what would you want to do on:

Your birthday?
Christmas Eve?
Thanks Giving?
Valentine's Day?
Easter?
Halloween?
Fourth of July?
Our Anniversary?

# 360

How many different sex positions can you think of in 30 seconds? How many do you think we can perform in one minute?

# 361

If we were on a nature walk and came to a secluded meadow next to a large tree, where would you most like to have sex?

A: Hanging onto the branches up in the tree
B: On the soft lush green grass

# Randy Readers

*Start an erotic reading circle for women only. Read delicious passages of erotic literature and porn out loud. Indulge in chocolate truffles and champagne while stimulating exotic fantasies and adventurous ideas for wild, passionate sex. Safely practice talking dirty as an expression of your sexuality. Become a randy reader then enjoy hot sex with your lover.*

# 362

If we were to play out a fairy tale fantasy scenario, what kinds of erotic role playing scenarios can you think of based on any characters, scenes or settings found in:

Little Red Riding Hood?
Peter Pan?
Snow White?
Cinderella?
Sword and the Sorcerer?
Arabian Nights?
Beauty and the Beast?
Robin Hood?
Alice in Wonderland?
Your favorite story?

# 363

In your favorite erotic stories or fantasies, do you identify mostly with the dominant or submissive characters? What types of settings, roles or activities turn you on the most?

# 364

In what ways could we use erotica to improve our sex life together? What forms of erotica do you find arousing?

# 365

When you think of some of your favorite stories, what kinds of erotic role playing scenarios can you imagine for us to try?

# 366

In a sci-fi fantasy or role playing scenario, would you rather be:

Star Trek or Star Wars characters?
Curious alien or human subject?
Exotic alien or human visitor?
Human or realistic sex robot?
Alien ruler or human "god"?

# 367

What historic period, location or event most inspires your erotic thoughts? What classic literature most inspires your erotic fantasies?

# Wild Fantasies

*A special costume can help you get in the mood for some very wild fantasies. Experiment mating as though you're different animals, fanciful creatures or even aliens. Your mind is the most potent sex organ you have. Let it run wild and free.*

## 368

If we could transform into two animals in heat for some wild sex, what species would you want to become and why?

## 369

What kinds of "adulterous" scenarios or fantasies would you consider role playing together?

## 370

What kinds of costumes have you ever had sex in? What would be your favorite costumes for either or both of us to wear while having sex?

## 371

If you were given a "free pass" weekend with absolutely no negative consequences, what sexual antics would you most want to indulge in?

## 372

If we were to play out different fantasy scenarios, how would you feel about role playing (fill in the blanks):

Sex slave being sold at auction in …?
Sex scientist and volunteer researching …?
A wild western involving …?
Farmer's daughter and stable boy in …?
Victorian style master and maid being …?

## 373

What kinds of same sex scenarios or fantasies can you imagine that involve either one or both of us? Are there any that you would consider role playing together?

## 374

What kind of erotic cartoon or animated fantasy can you imagine where we are the main characters? What characters would we each play?

## 375

If we were to get frisky together as "furries", what style and color of furry costumes would you choose for us to fool around in?

# Art of the Moan

*Men love women who moan as an expression of their passion. Oohs and aahs combined with some dirty words of encouragement add to the mental thrill. When your lover does something you like, moan to express appreciation and encourage more. Demonstrate your enthusiasm for each other whenever possible.*

# 376

How do you feel about sex play involving spanking, paddles or whips? Do you like to be spanked or would you prefer to be the one doing the spanking?

# 377

If we were to play out a mythical fantasy or role playing scenario, would you rather be the:

Angel or demon?
Sorcerer or enchanted?
Vampire or victim?
Genie or summoner?
Deity or worshiper?

# 378

If I pretended to be a life like sex doll that could only move when you move me, in what types of sex activities and positions would you use me to satisfy your desires?

# 379

If I told you I was bringing home some special candles for a night of hot sex, what thought would get you more excited:

A: Dripping hot wax on each other?
B: Making love in candle light?

# 380

Have you ever tried to have sex as quietly as possible? Have you ever purposely tried to make your sex play as loud as possible?

# 381

Have you ever had or would you like to have sex in a:

Cemetery?          Castle?
Historic site?          Church?

# 382

What was your experience like when you first:

Performed oral sex?
Received oral sex?
Had intercourse?
Had anal sex?
Used a sex toy?
Had an orgasm?

# Thrust Control

*In the missionary position, either partner can control the thrusting action. By varying the position of her legs, she controls the angle and depth of his thrusts. She can also wrap her legs around his waist and pull him tightly to her. By altering his thrusts from shallow to deep or slow to fast, he can create different sensations. Use thrust control to delay or activate launch.*

## 383

In what ways would you like to spice up our adult play so it's even more exciting and sexually thrilling?

## 384

What do you believe are the secrets to more and better female orgasms?

## 385

What do you consider the best position to avoid premature ejaculation?

## 386

If you had to come up with events for a sexual olympics competition, what kinds of "sporting" activities would you include? Try to come up with ten.

# 387

Are there any types of rough foreplay you would enjoy?

# 388

What types of furniture or household appliances have you had sex on or would like to have sex on? What creative sex positions can you imagine performing using the furniture we have?

# 389

If you were to place a sex ad in a local newspaper, what would it say?

# Sweet Surrender

*Surrender to the raw, primitive urges associated with a rear entry embrace. Explore the erotic possibilities of submission and dominance. She may feel seductively helpless as he opens her legs and ravishes her from behind. He may awaken his virile power as he thrusts deep inside her. Either way, let your lust fuel your passion and your fantasies.*

## 390

What is your favorite sex position and what do you like about it?

## 391

In a "forced sex" fantasy or role playing scenario, would you rather be the:

Kidnapper or hostage?
Prisoner or guard?
Pirate or captive?
Intruder or assaulted?
Conquerer or conquered?

## 392

What sex position creates the most intense type of orgasm for you?

## 393

Have you ever used a strap-on or double dildo with a girl or a guy (oral or anal)?

# 394

If we were to play out a "deflowering" fantasy scenario, how would you feel about role playing (fill in the blanks):

Virgins on our wedding night in …?
Teenagers holding off until …?
A fairy tale princess saved then …?
Young virgin initiated by …?
Ritual virgin sacrifice involving …?

# 395

Have you ever tried double or triple penetration with a real penis and a dildo or insertable vibrator? How do you feel about trying it together?

# 396

In a dominant/submissive type fantasy or role playing scenario, would you rather be:

Royalty or servant?
Master/Mistress or slave?
Pimp or prostitute?
Boss or employee?
Teacher or student?

## Backside Bliss

*With the woman on all fours and her legs slightly spread, the man kneels and enters her vagina with a backside view. Slowly, deliberately he slides his penis deep within her then withdraws it until the head is just about to slip out. Pause and repeat. With each slow, deep stroke, concentrate on every exquisite sensation. Close your eyes and allow your fantasies to lead you toward total bliss.*

## 397

How many different kinds of stimulating sensations can you think of lavishing on my bum?

## 398

What kinds of sex play do you think we could perform if we had to keep our butts cheek to cheek? What is the most contorted or acrobatic sex position you have ever tried? Would you try it again with me?

## 399

What is the strangest name you have ever heard for a sex position or activity? What creative names would you give to your favorite three sex positions?

# 400

What anal sex toys would you like to use with our sex play?

# 401

Although any sex is great exercise, which type of erotic fitness activity would you prefer doing in the nude?

A: Working out together with weights and gym equipment

B: Doing Tai Chi or Yoga

# 402

What is your favorite type of setting for:

Making love?
Enjoying oral sex?
Passionate fucking?
Having a quickie?
Self pleasuring?

# 403

Can sex still be good without any foreplay? In what situations would you forego foreplay and just have sex?

# Touch of Romance

*Give roses as a special romantic gesture and use them as a surprise sensual treat. Sprinkle rose petals on the sheets to create an enticing setting. Have your lover lie on the bed, close their eyes and focus on their sense of touch. Lightly stroke their body with a soft, velvety rose. Tickle and tease every delightfully erotic region of their body. Let them experience a Touch of Romance.*

# 404

What would your most romantic foreplay session involve?

# 405

What different touching techniques would you like to try?

# 406

What types of romantic gestures are most likely to get you in the mood to make love?

# 407

If you had to use a single color of paint to create a work of erotic art, what would it be? Can you describe the type of picture you would paint?

# 408

Imagine you discovered a sex genie and were granted three sex related wishes. What would you wish for if the wishes could only be applied to:

Yourself?
Me?
Everyone in the world equally?

# 409

What is the most erotically intriguing piece of art you've ever seen and why? How would you feel about searching for erotic art on the internet together? What kind of erotic art would you want in our bedroom?

# 410

What do you think about writing erotic letters or emails to each other? How romantic or dirty would you like them to be?

# 411

What is the most romantic trip or vacation you've dreamed about and what sexy activities would you like to do there?

# Frigid Fun

*On a hot summer day, increase your erotic heat with some Frigid Fun. Circle your nipples with an ice cube or popsicle. Once they're nice and perky, have your lover lick them with their hot tongue. Genitals also enjoy the sensual delight of this ice and tongue treatment. Explore other erogenous zones as well. Make each other shiver in anticipation.*

## 412

If we were both hot and sweaty, which sensual activity would you enjoy the most?

    A: Foreplay using ice then even hotter sex
    B: Making love in a cool shower

## 413

On a hot summer day, have you ever tried and would you like to try:

    Sex in the rain?
    Sex in a cool stream or water falls?
    Moonlight skinny dipping?
    Spending the day completely naked?
    Having sex outside under a tree?

## 414

Have you ever:

    Put a glass dildo in the freezer before using it?
    Made and used an ice dildo?
    Used ice while performing oral sex?
    Had sex outside in the snow?
    Made an erotic snow or ice statue?

# 415

Have you ever been involved in an orgy or visited a sex club? Would you like too?

# 416

What's the craziest and most memorable thing that happened to you while having sex?

# 417

Have you ever had or would you like to have sex:

On a roof?
In a tower?
Under a bridge?
In a tunnel?
On a mountain?
In a cave?

# 418

What is the most intriguing term you've heard for a kinky sex or fetish activity?

# Flicker & Flame

*Ignite her lust. Pretend your hot, wet tongue is a fluttering, licking flame. Never lingering on any spot, it flickers hot and fast around her inner thighs, labia and clitoris. When she is hot with desire, ultra lightly flick your tongue tip rapidly up, down and around her clitoris. Delicately concentrate your flame until she explodes in orgasm.*

## 419

What is one tip, technique or idea that you would like me to try to make oral sex even better for you?

## 420

What position do you prefer or find most comfortable for:
Performing oral sex?
Receiving oral sex?

## 421

How do you feel about using a vibrator or dildo to enhance cunnilingus?

## 422

If there was a lull in our sex life, how would you re-ignite our sexual desire for each other?

## 423

What new sex toys would you like to buy? What's the most expensive sex toy you own? What's the least expensive?

## 424

What is your favorite erotic video and what aspects of it do you like the most?

## 425

Have you ever named a sex toy after one of your lovers, a famous person or someone you lusted after? Which toy and what name did you give it?

## 426

What kinds of same sex scenes in fantasy, stories or porn turn you on?

# Supremely Satisfied

*In the euphoric state of exhaustion following physically passionate sex, every muscle in your body will feel relaxed and stress free. When you are supremely satisfied, let yourself float into a blissful sleep to replenish your body, mind and spirit. Cultivate your fantasies as you dream peacefully and contented.*

## 427

How do you feel about the quantity and quality of sex in our relationship?

## 428

How long would you say was the longest lasting orgasm you've ever had?

## 429

Have you ever had sex involving a penis that was bigger than your largest dildo or insertable vibrator?

## 430

Have you ever performed Kegel exercises to help strengthen your orgasms? Have you ever done them while having intercourse?

# 431

How do you achieve your most intense orgasms?

# 432

If we could somehow become virgins again fully believing we both have never had sex before (hypnosis, hymen reconstruction, etc.), would you want to do it? How do you think we could recreate the feelings of our first times having sex?

# 433

What other kinds of sex toys have you used other than vibrators and dildos? What's the best sex toy you've ever tried?

# 434

What kind of erotic story or fantasy can you think of that is set:

In a jungle paradise?
In a desert oasis?
On a topical island?
On a country estate?
Under a full moon?
On an alien planet?
In ancient times?
In a mystical place?

# Sensual Massage

*Massage virtuosos don't just give great massage, they experience it as a sensual connection. For greater intimacy, your lover should be nude. Hands are erogenous zones packed with sensitive nerve endings that love the feel of skin. Close your eyes to attune yourself to the sensual, delightful pleasures your lover is experiencing. Both of you will feel fantastic.*

## 435

What parts of your body do you most enjoy getting massaged? What part of your body would you most like me to massage with warm oil right now?

## 436

When does foreplay end and sex begin? Can intercourse be part of foreplay?

## 437

In what creative ways can you imagine pleasuring each other using:

    Silk ties or panties?
    A string of pearls?
    Kitchen utensils?
    Painting supplies?
    Chromed chains?

# 438

Although it's all fun for both of us, what types of sensual activities do you enjoy performing as foreplay mostly:

For your pleasure?
For my pleasure?

# 439

What do you feel are the male and female responsibilities in foreplay?

# 440

Of things we do or have done, what one foreplay activity or technique would you say:

Turns you on the most?
Gets me most excited?
Leads to sex the fastest?
Is the kinkiest?

# 441

For someone of the opposite sex that you find attractive, how would you describe the perfect:

Lips?            Eyes?
Chest?           Legs?
Ass?             Genitals?

# Waves of Pleasure

*More intense orgasms can be created by repeatedly building the arousal just to the brink and then slowing down or altering the type of stimulation. Keep the arousal burning but don't let it get out of control until you want it to. When your lover is beyond ready, push them over the edge. Give them an earth shuddering orgasm with tidal waves of pleasure.*

# 442

Have you ever experienced a female ejaculation? What is the wettest you've ever made the bed during sex?

# 443

Have you ever had or would you like to have sex:

On the deck of a boat?
On the beach?
In an ocean?
On a dock or pier?
On a raft?
On a waterbed?

# 444

What items would you want included in a pleasure chest that gets stranded with us on an exotic tropical island? If you were stranded alone on the island, what sex toy would you want to have with you?

# 445

Where and when did you last go skinny dipping? Where and when would you be willing to go skinny dipping with me?

# 446

If we were stranded on a deserted island, where would you most like to make love?

A: On the warm sand of the beach
B: In the calm ocean waters of a lagoon

# 447

If you had to classify the different types of orgasms you have experienced, how many categories would there be and what would be the differences?

# 448

Have you ever had or would you like to have sex in a:

Sand dune?
Tropical jungle?
Grassy meadow?
Lush forest?
Stable or hayloft?
Blooming orchard?

## Pussy Pleasuring

*Lightly lick her inner thighs. With your hot, moist tongue, delicately tease her lips open. Twirl your tongue over her clitoris briefly then flick the tip teasingly just in the opening of her vagina. Return to her clitoris using the underside of your tongue very lightly. Make her pussy purr with a gentle and rhythmic swirling, flicking, figure eight or circle motion.*

## 449

What was the best oral sex technique performed on you?

## 450

How would you describe your orgasm to someone who has never had one? How do you think male and female orgasms compare?

## 451

Do you prefer vaginal or clitoral orgasms? What do you think is the best sex position for having female vaginal orgasms?

## 452

If I was to play as your love pet, what type of animal would you want me to be? What kind of pet would you want to play for me?

# 453

What can I do to improve the pleasure you get from performing oral sex for me?

# 454

Do you prefer the look or feel of hairy, trimmed or fully shaved genitals on:

A man?
A woman?

# 455

What is the most embarrassing or funniest sex related event that you can remember that involved an animal?

# 456

In which sexually distracting situation would you get the most mischievous thrill?

A: Performing oral sex on me while I'm on the phone with my parents
B: Receiving oral sex while you are on the phone talking with your parents

# Finger Magic

*Use your fingers to get her to orgasm or primed for intercourse. Don't just concentrate on her clitoris. Rub her labia, vaginal opening and perineum. Slowly slip in a moist finger. Massage the opening to her vagina. Explore rather than thrust. Ask her if she wants if faster, harder or deeper. Works like magic.*

## 457

How do you most enjoy being touched during foreplay?

## 458

If you were magically given the ability to perform any special erotic trick with any part of your body, what would you want it be? What ability would you choose for me?

## 459

Do you prefer sex toys for G-spot or clitoral orgasms?

## 460

What kinds of role playing scenarios can you imagine the two of us doing together?

# 461

In what ways can you think of using a timer or stop watch in our sex play?

# 462

What do you think are the differences in sexual skills between a prostitute and a high priced escort?

# 463

What sorts of pain play would you like to experiment with?

# 464

In what ways have you ever used more than one dildo or vibrator at the same time? What combinations of sex toys do you find work best?

# Advanced Foreplay

*Many people view foreplay as a means to warm up prior to intercourse. Take it to the next level. Tantalize each other's minds and bodies well in advance of any sexual contact. Arouse erotic excitement as you tease each other with sexy suggestions or tender touches. Advance your foreplay hours or days ahead of time as you stimulate desire with creative games of love.*

## 465

What forms of "mental foreplay" help you get in the mood for sex?

## 466

What could I do that would make you fantasize all day about having sex with me?

## 467

How do you feel about using text or instant messaging to flirt with each other?

## 468

Have you ever engaged in cyber sex with a lover as foreplay before having sex?

# 469

Would you like to get together for 69 now and savor slow and sensual oral sex until we melt in ecstasy?

# More Sexy Ideas

We hope you're always on the look out for ways to enhance your relationship and spice up your love life. We believe a vibrant sex life is essential to maintaining a healthy and happy relationship. It's also a vital aspect of your personal well being. The shared intimacy and pleasures of lovemaking is something we all need. But we also crave passion and excitement to keep us feeling more alive. Satisfy your desires by continuing to learn about and experiment with creative ways to make sex wildly fun, exciting and thrilling together. Challenge each other to step out of your sexual comfort zone and explore your full erotic potential.

Come visit **www.sexquestionsforcouples.com** to discover more sexy questions and ideas for couples on our blog. We also run a number of other blogs and websites that you may find interesting:

- www.couplesgames.net
- www.friskyforeplay.com/ideas
- www.adultboardgamedesign.com
- www.frisky-sexual-fantasies.com
- www.sexysuggestions.com

If you have an iPhone or iPad, check out our two creative sex apps currently available in iTunes. Just do a search for:

- iLoveRandomSex
- Succulent Expressions

Made in United States
Troutdale, OR
08/16/2023

12134560R00080